EDGE BOOKS

LIBRARY OF WEIRD

THE WORLD'S
ZANIEST
SPORTS

by Tim O'Shei

raintree
a Capstone company — publishers for children

Raintree is an imprint of Capstone Global Library Limited, a company incorporated in England and Wales having its registered office at 7 Pilgrim Street, London, EC4V 6LB – Registered company number: 6695582

www.raintree.co.uk
myorders@raintree.co.uk

ISBN 978 1 4062 9206 0
18 17 16 15 14
10 9 8 7 6 5 4 3 2 1

British Library Cataloguing in Publication Data
A full catalogue record for this book is available from the British Library.

Editorial Credits
Aaron Sautter, editor; Kyle Grenz, designer; Charmaine Whitman and Katy LaVigne, production designers; Pam Mitsakos, media researcher; Kathy McColley, production specialist

Photo Credits
Corbis: Demotix/Graham Lawrence, 11; Dreamstime: Steve Gould, cover; Getty images: Hulton Archive/Newsmakers/Sean Dougherty, 14, Photodisc, 29; Landov: Reuters/ALEX GRIMM, 19; Newscom: REUTERS/SCOTT AUDETTE, 28, A3471 Boris Roessler Deutsche Presse-Agentur, 16, EPA/KARL PROUSE, 13, REUTERS/CATHAL MCNAUGHTON, 4–5, Splash News/Michele Eve, 17, picture-alliance/dpa/Frank Leonhardt, 23, REUTERS/WOLFGANG RATTAY, 25, WENN/CB2/ZOB, 8, 20, WENN Photos/WAAA/ZDS, 15, Itar-Tass Photos/Dzhavakhadze Zurab, 22; Shutterstock: Ariel Bravy, 21, Magnum Johansson, 10, Karel Tupy, 27, Chris Turner, 26, Velychko, back cover; Wikimedia: Tscheipi, 6, DavidUnderwater, 7, Pedroromero2, 9, gomattolson, 12; Wikipedia: Theredrocket/en.wikipedia, 24

Design Elements
Shutterstock: AridOcean, Kid_A (throughout)

Printed in China by Nordica
1214/CA21401620

CONTENTS

SLIMY, SLIPPERY
CHEESE-CHASING SPORTS!

Some people delight in hitting a hole in one or scoring a try. Others love the roar of the crowd. Whatever the reason, many people enjoy the thrill of competing in sport. They get a rush from scoring goals or being the first across the finish line. They love to compete, and they love to win.

But for some athletes, "normal" sports such as football or tennis aren't enough. Simply playing rugby or cricket doesn't excite them. Not even a death-defying sport such as skydiving is thrilling enough for some people.

These people seek out sports that are unusual, dangerous or just plain weird. Some people compete by swimming through a smelly, muddy **bog**. Others enjoy running down a steep hill while chasing a wheel of cheese. And some people have fun wrestling in a pool of gravy or racing against a horse!

BOG SNORKELLING

At the World Alternative Games, athletes do a unique type of snorkelling as part of a **triathlon**. Competitors **snorkel** through stinky, muddy water in a peat bog that looks like a thick chocolate milkshake!

bog type of wetland that includes wet, spongy ground and pools of muddy water

triathlon long-distance race made up of three parts, usually including swimming, cycling and running

snorkel tube used to allow a person to breathe under water

You'll find zany sports like these and many others in this book. Don't try them on your own – you could get hurt. But feel free to gasp, cringe or even laugh at the following crazy competitions!

CHAPTER 1

SPORTS WITH A TWIST

Surfing. Wrestling. Boxing. You might think of these as "normal" sports. But what if they include dogs, gravy or chess? When you add unusual elements to common competitions, they become totally wacky!

OCTOPUSH

Octopush is a fast and furious game of hockey – played under water! This unique sport was invented in the UK in the 1950s and is now played worldwide. Players take big gulps of air through snorkels before diving to the bottom of a pool. They then use a 30.5-centimetre spatula to move a 1.2 kilogram puck along the pool floor.

UNICYCLE HOCKEY

In a silent film from 1925, a comic actor on a **unicycle** crumpled a sheet of newspaper into a ball. Then he dropped it on the ground and started batting it around. He was trying to make people laugh, but without knowing it, he also inspired the game of unicycle hockey. Today many teams across Europe, Asia and Australia ride up and down playing this unique form of hockey.

UPSIDE-DOWN OCTOPUSH

For some people, playing hockey under water still isn't hard enough. Instead, they play an upside-down version in ice-covered water! Players first dive through a small hole in the ice, and then move a floating puck against the underside of the ice. It's cold and extremely dangerous. Players can lose track of where the air hole is and sometimes have to hold their breath for far too long.

unicycle *vehicle with a saddle and pedals like a bicycle, but with only one wheel and no handlebars*

GRAVY WRESTLING

Would you jump into a pool of gravy and wrestle another person for two minutes? At the World Alternative Games – some people do just that! Gravy wrestlers earn points and win matches based on audience applause for their moves. And in this crazy sport, the messier you get the better!

CHESS BOXING

First make your move … then throw a punch! Chess boxing combines the mental game of chess with the bruising sport of boxing. The first chess boxing match took place in London in 1978. Since then this unusual sport has spread to several other countries, including Germany and the United States. Inside a ring, two people square off for a round of chess, followed by a round of boxing. It's back and forth between the two sports until someone wins with a **knockout**, a **checkmate** or a judge's decision.

knockout *victory in which a fighter's opponent is unable to get up after being knocked to the ground*

checkmate *chess move in which an opponent's king cannot escape*

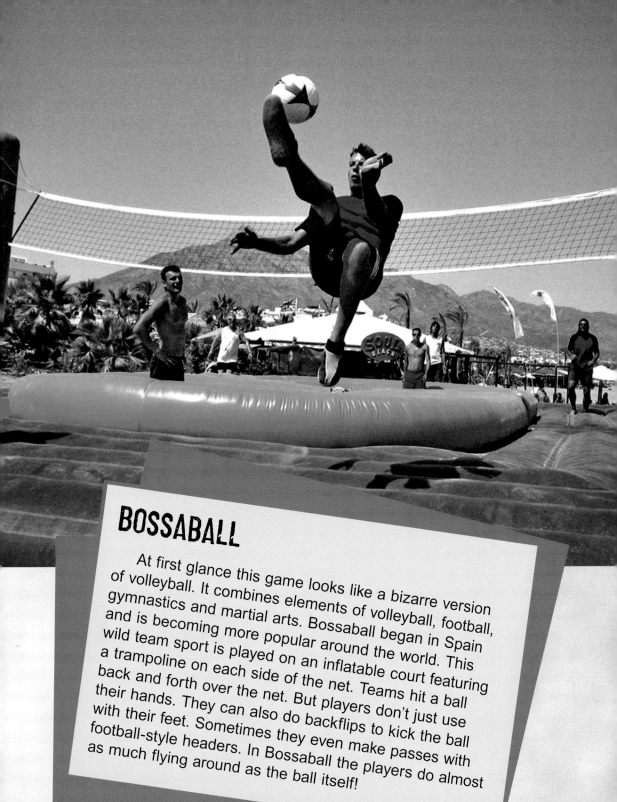

BOSSABALL

At first glance this game looks like a bizarre version of volleyball. It combines elements of volleyball, football, gymnastics and martial arts. Bossaball began in Spain and is becoming more popular around the world. This wild team sport is played on an inflatable court featuring a trampoline on each side of the net. Teams hit a ball back and forth over the net. But players don't just use their hands. They can also do backflips to kick the ball with their feet. Sometimes they even make passes with football-style headers. In Bossaball the players do almost as much flying around as the ball itself!

DOG SURFING

Did you know that some dogs can surf? Dog surfing is a new sport that's starting to appear at surfing spots around the world. Dogs usually wear life jackets and ride on 1.8- to 2.4-metre foam boards. Many dogs surf on their own, while others get on better with a human helper.

LIMBO SKATING

Limbo is a popular activity around the world. People compete to see who can lean backwards and duck under a pole without falling to the ground. But in countries such as India and China, people often compete in a very different version of this game. Limbo skaters do splits and lean forward to get as low to the ground as possible. Then they skate under objects such as cars. Limbo skaters are almost always children because they're shorter and more flexible than adults.

MAN VS HORSE MARATHON

Which is faster – a man or a horse? People in Wales have been trying to answer this question since 1980 with the yearly Man vs Horse Marathon. This 35-kilometre race takes place through the hilly Welsh countryside. Horses are normally faster on flat land, but they can't climb rocky cliffs the way human athletes can. It's a yearly gamble to see who will win: the human or the horse.

CHAPTER 2

WACKY RACES

Don't trip! Don't fall! Don't drop your wife! In most races the goal is to cross the finish line first. But the following races require competitors to do a little bit more.

MILK CARTON BOAT RACES

Don't throw away those old milk cartons. Recycle them and turn them into a boat instead! Milk carton boat racing is a fun event in many places. Some of these simple boats include just a piece of plywood floating on rows of cartons. But others are more complicated and colourful. People often decorate their boats to look like pirate ships, castles or even floating dragons!

RACING IN BATHS

Contestants in Canada try to paddle bath-shaped boats around a marked course on the water. Most races have only one person per bath-boat. But in synchronized racing, two paddlers sit face-to-face in the bath. Together they try to row their bath through the course in the fastest time. If they sink they're out of the competition.

BUN CLIMBING

Watch as a group of climbers scramble up a 15-metre tower to gather as many buns as they can. Welcome to Hong Kong's Cheung Chau Bun Festival! The race once featured thousands of real sweet buns stuck on **bamboo** towers. But in 1978 one of the towers collapsed, severely injuring many people. The event was cancelled for several years. But it was revived in 2005 when event organizers made some changes. The towers are now made of steel and the buns are made of plastic. But the climb is still as crazy as ever!

bamboo *tropical plant with a hard, hollow stem*

STILETTO RACING

Both women and men can compete in this 55-metre dash in high-heeled shoes. Racers need to bring their own stilettos for these wild races that are held around the world. Each race has its own shoe rules. The heels are often a minimum of 7.6 centimetres tall and no more than 60 millimetres wide. All shoes must be open-toed and no boots are allowed. Winners of these bizarre races not only stand proud, but also stand tall!

WIFE CARRYING

Wife carrying competitions are a wacky part of several festivals around the world. Partners in this sport don't have to be married. People carry their partners on their backs through **obstacle courses** featuring sand, logs and water troughs. The winning team often wins twice the "wife's" weight in a cash prize.

obstacle course *type of racecourse with a series of obstacles that contestants must jump over, climb or crawl through*

CHEESE ROLLING

In one popular event in Gloucestershire, hundreds of people chase a bouncing 3.2-kilogram wheel of cheese rolling down a steep hill. Whoever catches the cheese gets to take it home as a prize. People often stumble, fall and roll down the hill in their efforts to catch the cheese. This event can be dangerous. Many contestants go home with cuts, bruises or even broken bones.

ROBOT CAMEL RACING

Camel racing is an old tradition in several Middle Eastern countries. In the past, riders were small, lightweight children. But conditions became too dangerous for children, so race organizers in Qatar came up with a solution. They built **humanoid** robots to ride the camels instead. The robots are controlled by joysticks.

humanoid having human form or characteristics

OFFICE CHAIR SLALOM

In an office setting, rolling around in a chair instead of walking might be considered funny or perhaps a bit lazy. But now it's a sport! In office chair **slaloms**, contestants sit in an office chair and race through a course using nothing but their feet to power them. In this race, if anyone stands up they're immediately **disqualified**.

slalom *race in which competitors race around obstacles*

disqualify *prevent someone from taking part in or winning an activity*

OUTHOUSE RACING

At one time a law in Virginia, USA, made outdoor toilets illegal. To protest the law, angry citizens pulled their outdoor toilets, called outhouses, into the streets. The Virginia law is long gone, but the idea of wheeling one's outhouse around remains. In the World Champion Outhouse Races, one person sits on the toilet while others push or pull the outhouse. It's a fun event that involves a lot of preparation. People paint and decorate the outhouses as if they're carnival floats.

GIANT PUMPKIN RACES

Think of all the things you can do with a pumpkin. You can eat it, carve it into a halloween lantern – or even turn it into a boat! For this popular race in Nova Scotia, Canada, people paddle huge pumpkin boats down a river. They make their boats out of giant pumpkins that often weigh more than 360 kilograms.

BED RACING

Don't expect a good night's sleep when you climb into one of these beds. In several festivals across the United States, racers work in teams to push beds down streets and around obstacles. Usually one person sits on the bed while the others push it along. Bed racers can decorate their beds, too. In one race, the beds were made to look like pirate ships!

CHAPTER 3
CRAZY CONTESTS

Have you ever been in a sword fight using cardboard tubes? Do you enjoy simple games such as rock-paper-scissors? Do you know anyone who has an amazing beard? You may not believe it, but crazy contests featuring everyday things such as these are found all over the world.

COMPETITIVE NETTLE EATING

In some parts of the world, hot dog and pie-eating contests are a common sight. But in Dorset, contestants gobble down leafy green stinging nettles! Stinging nettle leaves contain an acid that can make a person's mouth go numb. Because of this, the nettle-eating contest has a no-drooling rule. Having little drool shows that a person is a skilled nettle eater.

ROCK-PAPER-SCISSORS

Most people have played rock-paper-scissors at some point. But did you know that some people play the game as professionals? In the USA Rock Paper Scissors League (USARPSL), players take the game seriously. Competitors play in big tournaments with referees. Some players dress up in colourful outfits to impress the crowds. Professional players can even win cash prizes at official competitions.

WORLD BEARD AND MOUSTACHE CHAMPIONSHIPS

Have you ever seen a beard shaped like a castle? How about a moustache that coils like a snake? At the World Beard and Moustache Championships, facial hair is turned into a serious sport! Awards are given for many categories ranging from the most natural to the most creative. Beards and moustaches can be especially long or curl around in wild directions. Men even gain or lose points based on how well they use moustache wax and other styling products.

EGG ROULETTE

This crazy game is all about luck. Competitors first receive six eggs. The eggs are all hard-boiled, except for one. People take turns smashing the eggs on their own foreheads. The first unlucky person to get "yolked" is out of the game!

TOE WRESTLING

Toe wrestling started in a village in Derbyshire in 1976. Since then it's grown big enough to have its own world championship. Competitors first place a foot inside a shoebox-sized space called the "toedium". They then interlock their big toes and begin to wrestle. The first person to wrestle their opponent's foot to the ground two-out-of-three times is declared the winner.

PILLOW FIGHTING

In 2004 some people in Canada created a professional pillow fighting league. They combined elements of professional wrestling with the basic idea of bashing people with pillows. The women-only league didn't last long. But the tradition of pillow fighting lives on at sleepover parties!

FINGER JOUSTING

It's not polite to poke someone – unless you're a finger jouster! Opponents in this sport first lock their right hands together. They then extend their index fingers and try to poke each other as often as possible. Players twist, twirl and drop as they try to score points. They can even compete for the World Finger Jousting Championship!

PEA-SHOOTING

This is a simple sport, but it's serious business for some people. Players use a 30-centimetre pea-shooter to shoot dried peas at a target 3.7 metres away. Top competitors at the World Pea Shooting Championship take the sport to another level. The distances get longer, and pea-shooting tubes start to look like something from a science-fiction film. World champion shooter George Hollis even added a laser-guided sight to his pea-shooter for complete accuracy.

WORM CHARMING

At the World Worm Charming Championships, contestants earn points based on the number of worms they can lure out of the ground in a certain amount of time. The most popular trick is to stick a garden fork into the ground and strike it. The vibrations make worms think a predator, such as a mole, is moving towards them. They wiggle their way to the surface, where worm charmers gather them to earn points.

CARDBOARD-TUBE FIGHTING

Witness an epic battle between two fierce competitors! Each fighter wields a deadly – cardboard tube? Sword fighting is made safer in the sport of cardboard-tube fighting. Contestants duel with metre-long cardboard tubes. Rules of the Cardboard Tube Fighting League state that opponents can't stab or hit each other in the face. They also can't use their arms to block being hit. The winner is determined very simply – the first one to break their opponent's tube wins.

FISHERMAN'S JOUST

Row, row, row your boat. Just don't fall down! In France, Switzerland and Germany, teams of rowers paddle boats towards one another on a river. At the side of each boat stands a "jouster" with a shield and a lance. As the boats pass each other, the jousters try to knock one another into the water. The jouster who is left standing is the winner.

CAMEL JUMPING

Ready, set, go … and leap over a camel (or two, or three or six)! The Zaraniq tribe of Yemen created the unique sport of camel jumping. Each contestant gets a running start, jumps off a small dirt mound and hurdles over camels lined up side-by-side. If any part of a jumper's body touches a camel, he's out. After every successful jump, one more camel is added to the line until a winner is declared.

CHAPTER 4

TO THE EXTREME!

Running, jumping and skating are common activities many people do every day. But those sports aren't thrilling enough for some people. They take their sport to the extreme by adding mud, electrical wires, giant hamster balls – or even ironing boards!

EXTREME SKYDIVING

Normal skydiving already seems crazy to some people. But extreme skydivers take the sport to a whole new level. While wearing special gliding suits, they fly like missiles at up to 161 kilometres an hour. These daring jumpers often sail as little as 4.5 metres above the mountain slopes!

EXTREME IRONING

There are few household jobs as dull as ironing. But in extreme ironing, athletes combine ironing with extreme sports. Some people iron a shirt while skydiving or iron trousers after climbing to the top of a mountain. Others do their ironing while **rappelling** down a cliff!

rappel *descend down a rock face using a strong rope*

EXTREME MUD RUNS

Running is tough. Running through mud is tougher. But some runners take things to the extreme. They challenge themselves by running through mud, fire, ice and other obstacles. Tough Mudder and Tough Guy competitions are often held in Europe, Australia, New Zealand and North America. In these extreme competitions, athletes battle their way through difficult courses. They climb rope ladders, plunge into ice baths, sprint through fire and squirm through mud pits. Sometimes they even wiggle their way through live electrical wires! Contestants often have to sign legal documents recognizing that the course is dangerous and that they might get injured.

ZORBING

Zorbing allows people to imagine what it's like to be a hamster! One or two people climb inside a giant air-filled ball called a Zorb. They then run inside like a hamster in a ball. Daring Zorbers roll down steep hills for an exciting thrill. Zorbing began in New Zealand, but has since become popular in several other countries. This wild sport can be fun, but also dangerous. People have been injured and even killed by slamming into trees or rolling off cliffs.

MOUNTAINBOARDING

Mountainboarding is a lot like snowboarding, but without the snow. Mountainboarders ride boards with heavy-duty wheels down rocky mountain slopes. Like snowboarders, they usually do stunts and tricks along the way. Mountainboarders often take part in "big air" competitions. They leap off a ramp and do as many tricks as possible before they land.

PARKOUR AND FREE RUNNING

Imagine being a powerful superhero. You could leap from rooftop to rooftop with the ground far below. You could hurdle over steep stairs or climb up walls like an insect. In cities around the world, parkour and free running athletes don't just imagine making these amazing moves – they do them! These athletes train hard to jump, somersault or climb over everything they see. They turn the world around them into their personal obstacle course.

POWERBOCKING

With a pair of powerbocks, not only can you run fast, you can also do amazing jumps and flips in the air. Powerbocks are basically short, spring-loaded stilts. Powerbocking is said to feel like running on pogo sticks or jumping on a trampoline. Skilled powerbockers can do high-flying stunts and appear to have almost superhuman powers. One powerbocker has even set a record by flipping backwards 20 times in 20 seconds!

QUIDDITCH

Author J.K. Rowling created the game of "Quidditch" in her Harry Potter novels. It became so popular that some fans have turned the game into a real-life sport. Quidditch teams are found across Europe, Australia and North America. Players run around a grass field while holding a broomstick between their legs. Three "chasers" try to kick and pass a ball through hoops to score goals. "Keepers" are similar to goalkeepers. They guard their team's hoops. Two "beaters" try to knock opponents out of the game by hitting them with a ball called a "bludger". Each team also has a "seeker" and a "snitch". The snitch is a person dressed in yellow with a tennis-ball "tail" attached at the waist. The seekers chase the snitches and try to grab their tails. Winning is based on scoring the most points or capturing the opposing snitch's tail, which automatically ends the game.

CRASHED ICE

Competitors in crashed ice races wear ice-skates, helmets and pads just like ice-hockey players. But this sport has nothing to do with hockey. In cities around the world where winter brings extreme cold weather, contestants race down ice-covered tracks. They crash and bash into each other while trying to be the first one to cross the finish line. Crashed ice is a difficult sport. Players often find it difficult to stay on their feet through the track's curves and unexpected jumps.

WATERCROSS

In the 1970s people in Wisconsin, USA, discovered that their snowmobiles could race on water as well as on snow. So they created a whole new sport for it! In watercross, snowmobilers twist and turn their vehicles at high speed on the open water. But there's one thing snowmobiles don't do well on water – float! If the machine slows down or tips over, it sinks.

KABADDI

Hold your breath! Kabaddi is popular in countries such as India and Pakistan, as well as other parts of Asia. This form of tag has two teams of seven players on each side of a court. A "raider" from one team has 30 seconds to run across the court and tag as many opponents as possible. However, the raider has to do this on only one breath of air! To make sure raiders don't cheat, they have to chant the word "kabaddi" the entire time they are raiding the other team.

UP TO THE CHALLENGE

From bed racing and camel jumping to Quidditch and Zorbing, people around the world compete in many wild and wacky sports. Whether daring, weird or downright dangerous, athletes enjoy meeting the challenges offered by the world's zaniest sports.

GLOSSARY

bamboo tropical plant with a hard, hollow stem

bog type of wetland that includes wet, spongy ground and pools of muddy water

checkmate chess move in which an opponent's king cannot escape

disqualify prevent someone from taking part in or winning an activity; athletes can be disqualified for breaking the rules of their sport

humanoid having human form or characteristics

knockout victory in which a fighter's opponent is unable to get up after being knocked to the ground

obstacle course type of racecourse with a series of obstacles that contestants must jump over, climb or crawl through

rappel descend down a rock face using a strong rope

slalom race in which competitors race around obstacles

snorkel tube used to allow a person to breathe under water

triathlon long-distance race made up of three parts, usually including swimming, cycling and running

unicycle vehicle with a saddle and pedals like a bicycle, but that has only one wheel and no handlebars

READ MORE

Extreme Athletes: True Stories of Amazing Sporting Adventurers (Ultimate Adventurers) Charlotte Guillain (Raintree, 2014)

Extreme Sports, Emily Bone (Usborne Children's Books, 2014)

Surviving Extreme Sports (Extreme Survival), Lori Hile (Raintree, 2012)

WEBSITES

www.gbuwh.co.uk
Find out more from the British Octopush Association, from the history of the sport to whether or not there is a junior club near you!

https://quidditchuk.org/
Learn more about real-life Quidditch and teams and events in the UK.

www.worldalternativegames.co.uk/
Learn more about bog snorkelling, wife carrying and other unusual sports. Look at photos and watch videos of all the action!

INDEX